T0151777

ALSO BY MATTHEW ROHRER

BOOKS

A Hummock in the Malookas
Satellite
Nice Hat. Thanks.
    (with Joshua Beckman)
A Green Light
Rise Up
Gentle Reader!
    (with Joshua Beckman and Anthony McCann)
A Plate of Chicken
Destroyer and Preserver
Surrounded by Friends
The Others

CHAPBOOKS

They All Seemed Asleep
A Ship Loaded with Sequins Has Gone Down

AUDIO CDS

Adventures While Preaching the Gospel of Beauty
    (with Joshua Beckman)

THE SKY CONTAINS THE PLANS

MATTHEW ROHRER

WAVE

BOOKS

SEATTLE

AND

NEW YORK

THE
SKY
CONTAINS
THE
PLANS

Published by Wave Books

www.wavepoetry.com

Copyright © 2020 by Matthew Rohrer

Wave Books titles are distributed to the trade by

Consortium Book Sales and Distribution

Phone: 800-283-3572 / SAN 631-760X

Library of Congress Cataloging-in-Publication Data

Names: Rohrer, Matthew, author.

Title: The sky contains the plans / Matthew Rohrer.

Description: First edition. | Seattle : Wave Books, 2020.

Identifiers: LCCN 2019030459

ISBN 9781950268054 (limited edition hardcover)

ISBN 9781950268047 (trade paperback)

Classification: LCC PS3568.O524.A6 2020 | DDC 811/.54—dc23

LC record available at https://lccn.loc.gov/2019030459

Designed by Crisis

Printed in the United States of America

9 8 7 6 5 4 3 2 1

First Edition

Wave Books 082

Sometimes I speak and I feel like it ain't my words

Like I'm just a vessel channeling inside this universe

—JOEY BADA$$

a gorgeous knot of words hovers before my face

when I fall asleep

—SUSIE TIMMONS

THE SKY CONTAINS THE PLANS

EVERYBODY'S RELATION TO CHANGE
IN THE SACK changes
as the very morning
falling on them through
the white curtain changes
the light grows older
in the trees outside
the bed settles in
like an old stairway
made of stones smoothed
where the bodies sleep
in a dream I had
I saw Time turning everything yellow
I saw many
other things of wonder
before I fell down
and rising
in the morning
the same woman is
sleeping next to me

THEN HE WAS THROWN
OUT OF ESPRESSO ROYALE
for calling the devil
up from a cup
of tea which failed
but terrified the manager
we all laughed we
only came to take
advantage of the day-
old pastries and drink
one endless teacup
his voice
as he put on his trench coat
was like a little sigh
from underneath a blanket
I've seen the devil
he shouted on his
way out his eyes looked weird
this was years ago
the devil never appeared
people continued
going to and fro
across the earth
posting their comments online

DID YOU EAT YOUR BLOSSOMS
ON TIME? I called out
to all the diners in a restaurant
made entirely of blossoms
singing beautiful
little snatches of songs
as I floated past
and when I awoke you were
entangled in me
and still asleep.
The lonely sound of a room at night
bent its strings to my ears.
In some cultures this is
a form of meditation.
The Chinese used to eat
blossoms until they vomited
halos of flowers
in the fields. But the silence
preceded me and surrounded
me. I lay perfectly still
wrapped around you,
an image of us in my mind
boating across all the wine
we've drunk together
in the slow turn of evening.

It will seem like nothing happened
a few more polkas disappeared

into the evening air
a deep breath inhaled the universe

and let it out again
when late May gets into

everything and everyone
feels a significant part

of what they have done
is dream—it will seem

like nothing happened
when the sky is blue

and indistinct, it will seem
like boating down a river

of flowers in an ensorcelled
city where everyone is veiled

it will seem like money will be
stripped of its crown

but that is the dream
that can't carry the day

WE PROBABLY SHOULDN'T BE
DISCUSSING THIS, it makes me

angry, the mental illnesses
of the hyperacquisitive

that pass for heaven's blessing
we shouldn't invite this

stuff into our home
I wash out the air

with the Smetana polkas
and drink a little ginger tea

because we decided not to
keep whiskey in the house

this month to see
what would happen

and it's happened

THE ZIPPER-UPPER OR WHATEVER—
HERE'S YOURS. We'll need
this and many more
accoutrements for our
assault on our dreams.
I have already packed the salami.
What we can carry
with us is only limited
by how deeply we sleep. In a
dark river beneath our bed
a current carries off our cares.
And floods them back on us.
We seek its source. We want a snack.
The ease with which we walk
these foreign streets
is fleeting. Under dark-colored
skies we sit down to eat our bread.
The feeling is incomplete.
The things we want in dreams
are all right here.

THIS IS MY CHALLENGE TO YOU,
she said, laying a severely
wounded crab on the table
between us. And walked away.
And slammed the door. And
turned on the car. And
drove away. The situation
was hopeless, and I was
nothing, I was just one
blade of grass on the prairie.
If she really thought I could
put our crab back together
she would have stayed to
watch. She would have
leaned over me while I
worked, her hands
on my chair. She would
have turned on a little music.
Instead I have to choose
the music. A plane flies
overhead. I know it's her.
All night the moon makes
a little sound.

CONSERVE-A-LAWYER
is the name
of the company
she said sweetly
outside the tavern
in a mist
I don't understand
what it's for
Conserve-a-Lawyer
I told her
she kissed me
I know that
she told me
it's not important
what you know
you're not paid
to understand things
but I said
Conserve-a-Lawyer?
they don't need
to be saved
they're all over
driving shiny cars
down my street
much too fast

they have ads
on the subway
she just laughed
while she drank
a blue cocktail
then got in
a sleek vehicle
that lifted off
and hovered there
over the neighborhood
which she littered
with some wrappers
then the thing
seemed to melt
and was gone
and never returned

THEY KIDNAPPED ALABAMA
to prove a point

the new map was made
of spiderwebs covered with dew

the terrible history of Alabama
fit into an envelope

all the state troopers
drove away in tears

the mirrors stopped reflecting
good times

all the while hidden
where it used to be

under the same name
down by the sea

I WISH A FIRE WOULD
DESTROY THAT WHOLE
NEIGHBORHOOD SO THEY
COULD START OVER
with damselflies
and a mountain stream
that talks that sings
in different voices
and the birds punctuate
their grief with pip-squeaks
in far-off thunder
the last time I was there
a spider bit me on the leg
everyone sat around watching
me on their venomous televisions

It's under oath
that a book
can make you
want to hit
your best friend
in his face
it's under oath
she told me
while I buttoned
up my pants
to live zealously
can also mean
denying yourself things
I said what
does that mean
she told me
about a dream
in the woods
the low drone
of a vehicle
in the night
coming this way
I waited awhile
but she said
that was it

I felt cold
on the back
of my neck
the little hairs
were standing up
I can't say
exactly how come
I just felt
like I was
in a tent
I could see
was literally crawling
with spiders

YOU DON'T THINK THERE'S
GOING TO BE A WORLD
OF MOTION in the trees
but then a tree falls
cracking, no wind, a foggy
night on the road
you don't expect a fire
to rush across the sky
and leave a scar
you can see as you walk
down the hillside
but there it is, a line
across the night
from Arcturus to
West Virginia
and a ground fog building
up all around
a mist over the creek
like in a fairy tale
and all the voices of the creek

SLAM THE WORD TO MAKE
IT PRETTY it isn't your word
it comes from the evening
it falls lightly like a little rain
and you can break it
and you can drink it
it is colorless and tasteless
without you, you should
chop it down and watch it
lie there moss growing on it
as it comes apart slowly
in the evening rain

WE WAITED IN HIS PLANT
NOW 2 TO 2
I said he's
not coming back listen
to that thunder he's long gone
the huge steel sliding doors
agreed with me they sang
a profound song of finality
closing on us leaving us
trapped in the belly
of the city to struggle out through
a sweatshop and blink at sunset
on the quay all four
of us untouched
in our hearts by this
and we returned
to the bar where the famous
poet sat by the door
and was kind to us

You're consuming darkness
she told me
I knew it
I was talking
far too much
I was taking
the darkness in
and giving it
all out again
there's no reason
to do it
I realized this
I was sitting
in one place
while spiders crawled
all over me
or I said
too many things
that were easily
replaced with silence
like a shot
I wanted to
spring out across
the treetops
in love with everyone

I heard thunder
and saw lightning
move in slowly
down the valley
and I didn't
feel the least
bit tempted to
plunge a knife
into a critic

ONE NAVY PAINTING
of an armored butterfly
says it all

follow the money
to the mouth
of the liar

he will be killed
by his own comrades
in a courtroom

how lovely it is
to watch the trees
visibly shaken

WHERE ARE MY OTHER PLANETS?
is the title of a painting by a guy
who lives across the street
whose name I don't know
but who is famous
or perhaps infamous
on the street because
he is a baiter of bears
and who often staggers
up the wrong stoop
at night, drunken, cursing
smelling of bear grease
it's agreed there's no excuse
for this the stoops are only similar
in that they're stoops
and once I was parking my car
when another neighbor started talking
to me about this baiter of bears
he called him a clown and a jackass
he's also a painter I said
which made me sound like I was defending him
it's just that I accidentally saw his painting
in a gallery where I had gone
to hear the revolution espoused
and it sounded good
but then we all went home
and forgot to revolt

IT'S NOT LIKE I HAVE HIS
DEATH ON MY FOOT
I just stepped on his
vegetarian sausage
and he went off
to pout and tell on me
days ago and quite
by accident here I am again
on the sidewalk where this all
went down staring at
the flattened sausage
the bright sun flickering
across it, dried out, nearly
a different color and sometimes
when I see something like that
a pile of dog shit in the park
or vomit outside a bar
I think: what if I ate that?
I briefly imagine it.
I have no idea why.
I don't want to.

You've got a hollow look
on your face she said

I was thinking of mustard gas
eating at the lungs of people

trapped on a ship floating
adrift on the sea

which I'd read about
over someone's shoulder

on the subway at least
I think that's what it said

I don't want any more news
but I can't turn away

she said you need some sun
so I took a walk

in the park, it was full
of babies being pushed

along in elegant transits
down all the paths

the obvious thing would
have been to envy them

but I really thought about it
and I enjoy walking

THE ROCKING HORSE SAID FAMILY
DESIRE outweighs personal
desire. It was completely dark
in the room, the middle
of the night. The boy opened his eyes
wide and his heart beat crazily.
There was an indistinct loudness
in his ears that made him feel
cut off from the world.
From what was happening.
Which was that after years
of silence, the rocking horse
in the corner of his room had spoken.
The boy wasn't even sure
what it had said had been meant
for him. As the silence continued
and the rocking horse failed
to say anything further, the boy
relaxed. His eyes adjusted
to the dark. The rocking horse
looked exactly the same.
The night kept rolling
across the land and eventually
passed over.

NEVER LIGHTS AS DIM AS SARA

never sky as harrowed

never waves as tucked in

never paths across the lawn as uninspiring

never tree as gauchely flowered

never the ground littered as neatly

never a little petal so delicate

THE CANOE IS NOT
SITTING UP BY ITSELF

something is holding it we
cannot see, something moves

rushing through the early
summer afternoon under

clouds and wakes the baby
too soon she looks shocked

the birds sound frantic
unless they are all in love

a feeling comes to the river
where the boats go slowly

pulled against the rowers'
straining by a great dark

muscle below them
on a sunny day

with dark blue clouds
gathered around

it is a terror to be out even
on small water alone

HE FELL ON HIS ASS
HE MIGHT HAVE BEEN CAPTURED

we left him there
we didn't stop to see

what they did to him
we fled through the park

with the blue light all over
us from the helicopters

until the sky cleared
and we stopped at a diner

for a coffee and grappa
while the cops hurried past

a baby was crying
that no one would tend to

and after awhile
we got up and left

the night was too clear
all the stars were on trial

I went to the subway
and they took 2 taxis

our parting was downplayed
the whole city's a camera

and we're all the actors
Shakespeare was right

but this is much grimmer
than what he imagined

WHAT SHALL I DO 42-71?
The sun is a cruel master

72-81 is too much
for me not to notice it

to push against it a little
while still thinking

about William Carlos Williams
writing "The Yachts" 71-72

thought almost does feel
physical, a fluid

as the ancients thought
without benefit of electric fans

but only take me away sunrise
to sunset, they didn't have numbers

but leave the evening to me
it is where I belong

Bless my nameless hour
with red wine where
you are now
well lit in a sunny
outdoor tavern that looks
over all three rivers
whether there really are three
or whether one river
flows into another
the facts are with science
but not blessing
and I want your blessing
the whole town's blessing
by spilling red wine on your lips
and kissing your idea
of me because I'm
home with the kids

Yesterday could do a better
job of explaining that than I could.
The mist pulls away from the bridge
and there's a body. Lying twisted
out of its boots. In a very sophisticated
pose. And the streets are strewn
with dried beans. You can talk
about how it works afterward
but it works or it doesn't.
Two women wash some clothes
through a hole in the ice.
A nonviolent demonstration
of the birds alights in the frozen vines.
It is a success.

THE COUGHING BRINGS ME BACK
TO LEVEL ONE. I open my eyes.
The buildings are rubble.
The only people there are
wrapped around themselves.
Level one is acrid, the sound is whispers.
The color is broken. I switch
to level two. They worship
the flowers. They bear them
to the festival where the children
are already kneeling.
The horses are restrained
behind the dark leaves.
Level two is oppressive. I leap
to my death on level three,
where tall elegant ladies
cannot stand me.

IF YOU SAW ME YOU'D
BE SWALLOWED BY A YELLOW BUS
and regurgitated as flowers
but I am hidden in
the sky I am hidden in peace
if you looked into my mirror
you wouldn't see yourself
as thin white rips through red
nightmares as I see myself
a gaunt figure beckons you
but he is awful you run
you stumble in your coat
down the path I watch you
I watch everyone passing by
it is painful seeing
how uncomfortable everyone is

So now I determine she was a selective victim

I was too distracted
to notice how she fluttered

across the street dressed
like an old stack of newspapers

I just saw her walking
to the neighbor's to hang out

in the back each night laughing
in the continuous blue light

that never foreclosed on us
I heard all their laughs rise up

like waves behind the house
and wrongly felt comforted

that I knew where she was
when the truth was darker

there was something wrong
with me after all

IT WAS NICE TO SLEEP
WITH HIM AS A YOUNG
GIRL she told us again
we had enough material now
but couldn't seem to leave her apartment
the hard candies actually emitted little haunting tones
that held us there frozen
though our minds wanted out
into the hallway and down
into the street
but we couldn't get up
and she wouldn't stop talking
about sleeping with him then
when a strapless dress cost
the same as two tangerines
and most of the girls
chose the tangerines but she
walked out one night dressed
like an unsheathed dagger shining
under the moon and he
saw her from his cab
took her back to Germany
and made her his queen under the mountain
put her in charge of the troll armies

the army of giants
bushes rising up against trees
the sea turning against the mountains
everybody somehow on her side

BUT WHEN YOU WERE COUNTING
YOU SKIPPED 6, 7 AND 8

she said. She looked
like a nun but wasn't

she was
I somehow understood
though I was only 8
empty
moving around the classroom
out of habit

her greatest gift
was to disappear

when she saw me
looking at her
this way
she sent me to the guidance counselor

I was the only person
for miles
without a television

I moved up
and down
seemingly by chance
in the world

I ended up in a book

ALL RIGHT SMELL YOUR FINGER-
nails—are the hot peppers
still there? A bird's shadow
suddenly peels across
the brick wall outside
the kitchen. If you don't wash
your hands now it's like
a river. You go on.
You can't go on.
Under a shadowy cloud.
When you snap your fingers
and the day fills the very
bottom of your lungs.
You learn the art of the
kitchen in the bedroom.
You learn the art of the bedroom
from your friends.

I VISUALIZED THAT IDEA LEAVING MY HEAD IN A BATHYSPHERE

it was a tidy farewell
I observed with a smile

I no longer remembered
what the idea was about

it swam away and I
remained there

the pleasures of bedtime
the imagination's sad flute

blowing down all the clover
in the park at night

A TOY SPACESHIP CALLED
ALMOND CHICKEN
vs. the Mega Gun. The Almond
Chicken wins. The Almond
Chicken vs. the Disasteroid.
The Disasteroid is victorious.
The unopposed Disasteroid rips
through the Earth.
The Earth is smashed into a billion
tears. The tears spread
out across the sky.
From each little piece
of the Earth a toy spaceship lifts off.
Revenge in its little heart.

My name is Tromas Neebar
my country of origin unimportant
tonight I come to tell
of marvelous wonders under stars
of fields of wildflowers shining
all night with strange lights

in the daylight
an image of my face was pressed
into the wildflowers and grasses
and they pulled me out
of my seat at work
they brought me to see it
a huge cheer rose up
into the morning though why
even they were not sure

who was I to be
a mysterious face pressed down
on the countryside? I worked
for a furniture reupholstery shop
on the night in question
I'd drunk an entire bottle
of whiskey but didn't die
I collapsed in my bathroom
I dreamed I was blooming

Spoken creases

come down

soft sound

late night

courtyard magnolia

old harpsichord

no wind

86 degrees

stoned shower

that's all

one fan

and shirtless

be calm

more silence

in here

she calls

POETRY CAN BE A WEAPON
OF WAR but only bad
poetry and you have to
stencil it on a bomb
drop it on a wedding
then you have a real war
on your hands and poems
like that can't be
seen clearly they hide behind
the bomb they're stenciled on
fall into the wrong hands
someone still has to report back
what the light looks like
spreading across the fields

BRIEF, ALMOST MICROSCOPIC
ATTEMPTS MADE ON MY LIFE

coming in from all sides
I swipe them away

I take the stairs up
into the afternoon 3 at a time

that was one of the most
pleasant subway rides ever

except that I was completely sober
I couldn't stop thinking

and when I wasn't thinking
I saw myself reflected in the window

holding my book
too close to my face

like everyone else
pretending to read

You look vintage
in the harpsichord
and window fan
with the sun's full
solstice foot up your ass
drinking a whiskey
and soda calling J
on the phone (not answering)
the time difference makes
you look even fatter
and marbled
you move
into a deeper slouch
the kids won't fall
asleep (too hot)
a new wrinkle
on your head
now that a little girl
is smiling at you

PRELINGUISTIC MYSTERY:
what do the animals think
about the weather? It must
disappoint them sometimes.
I'm thinking about birds.
How they have to fly.
How they get to fly.
Motherfuckers of luck.

As I STEP INTO THE CHAMBER
OF OUR IMAGINED LOVE
my mind goes blank. What
was it I saw here?
Two giantesses striding
toward me? For years I had
the strange belief that things
like feathers were filthy.
Then someone handed me
a striped feather, a hawk's,
and I woke up in a chamber
of bright clarity
from which I could see
how a June night at sunset
expands if you stare at it
and kind of swims in front
of your vision
and you can fall right into it

Seahorses are awesome
the entire ocean
is very beautiful
when it dances
in your eyes
typing a poem
on the shore
and it rises
into the air
to hang there
like another dimension
laid over this
Brooklyn June night
Prospect Park West
stunned into submission
just one color
in the sky
the traffic circle
typing a poem
without any paper
like the ocean
where the seahorses
move so unlikely
and the males
raise the young
the young burst
out of them

YOU WILL NOTICE A FAITHFUL
BLOCK OF CHEESE IS PRESENT

it cannot harm you
it doesn't even see you

or know that you're here
it is merely a bewitched cheese

that is faithful to me
and also does some typing

and filing, organizing really
it is an extremely wonderful cheese

do not be alarmed
I am its master

Hypoallergenic condominium
of excessive lyrical beauty, in the
center of a forest of crows, allergens,
and demons. I want to buy you
but I don't have the funds, or it would be more accurate
to say I don't have enough, and you sit there
pudgy and quiet, too good for anyone.

It's lovely at night inside when the rain falls.
All the empty rooms where no one is listening
even those have something alive about them.
There is something sort of sad about money.

But that isn't really the threat
of nostalgia, is it?
That's more like being allergic
to everything you used to do
which is weak.
A person without continuity
is broken off from himself
which is what you did.
That's how weak
you are. But you broke
in two. And a wolf chased you
out into the trees.
And treed you. And you
are treed.

BETWEEN WHOSE HUMAN ROCKS

I LAID my bleeding finger
while the sun stayed
in the sky past 10 o'clock
at night you wonder why I seemed
so distant I fell
asleep beside you each night
in a warm penumbra of love
is what I hoped you'd feel
from me not the sleep
I wrapped myself in
and hanged myself with
in dreams where I choked
on some future breath
I want everyone
in the world to know
I love your long legs

He seems lost
to a partisan girl.
He contemplates
a civilization beneath the waves
each evening. He drifts
across the water
in a low boat with no expression.

IT WAS ONE OF THE BLOOMING COMPLAINTS
OF MY CAMPAIGN
that you were not
more tremulous.
In the back of your car.
And what is lost
remains like the sunburn
of a placemat on a table.

THAT SEEMED VOLUMINOUS
floating there all night
with all the stars out
above us, Arcturus
motioning to us to go
home, go to bed, but we stayed
as long as we could
driving down to the parking lot
at the lake to see the stars
and lie across the hood of the car
and feel the hood still warm

TRY TO GO AWAY
AND LIE IN BED SIMULTANEOUSLY

it's like playing the trumpet
and making love

that's why I quit
before they made me join

the marching band
I knew the future was humid

nights all summer in the city
a woman with very long legs

a great feeling of freedom
even from our kids

sleeping nearby
slipping out of my body

to instruct the people of the world
about an esoteric

something or other
embracing them in my golden arms

with our truck parked
a few blocks away

in the rain and thinking
it can't stay parked there

tomorrow when they
sweep the street

IF YOU'RE GOING
TO BE A CHARMING
OFF-THE-TOP-OF-YOUR-HEAD
GUY, THEN DO YOUR WORK
he said, which made me
pause my upswing
and check the axe in my hands.
I don't remember saying
that I was, I said. He said I did, in my sleep,
almost every night. I said I had
a hard time believing him;
my concerns are solely with the body.
I almost never think of the mind
or even with it. Strictly authentic.
He said the authentic was like a vapor
in a Chinese painting: meant to obscure
what isn't even there. At which
I hefted my axe and slammed it
into a log that wouldn't split.
And it started to rain.

BUILDING UP TO IT
IS ACTUALLY BETTER
the morning is inexplicably cold
the forest is in concert
with a song fading out on the radio
on the drive up to the lake
the mind is only on the road
the clouds drag their knuckles
in the water
the summer
fills the mind
with an endless story
stretching in every direction
more impenetrable
than all the county's meth labs

I FOLLOW ART—IT GOES
PLACES AND I COME WITH IT
like a sparrow tossing
my head in the dust
and then hurrying to follow
the other identical sparrows

All the while thinking
I am the superior being
among all you sparrows
because you cannot see
what is inside me

It is a little victory
to keep that hidden

I WAS WARNED I MIGHT
BE LOSING HER
ANOTHER PEASANT
but I continued poling my skiff
away from the riverbank
with the peasant huddled
in the bow, transporting
him to, he claimed, an assignation
in the county seat
with a woman who owned a tavern
and knew the language of plants,
about which I was personally
concerned since I was all out,
so I agreed to ferry him
across after dusk
but began to suspect his true motive
as he covered himself in a sack
and shrank into the bilge.
She was still angry at me
for losing her farrier in the clouds
when I had him accompany me
last summer on a fruitless task.
Fruitless and secret and, tragically
for him, in retrospect entirely
without need of a farrier.

THEY'RE AN EMPTY SPACE
WHOSE INTRIGUE IS JUST THAT
they reflect you back.
I kept staring into them
while they passed me
on the street. Sometimes I sat
on the low steps of a shop
and tried to sketch them.
Then I always had lunch
in a public square with a designer waterfall
rushing down one of the walls,
whose intrigue was that
no matter how long I looked
into it I never saw anything
but water.

THIS HOME IS THE LIGHT
I always dreamed there'd be
in my home
a fleeting light you catch
a glimpse of in forests
late at night a light
that doesn't project itself much
into the world or seem
to care that much outwardly
and is the only thing
I can offer my kids

It is a secret joy
to be perceived as less
just taking up your own space
not projecting yourself out
into everyone else's
you know what I mean
you know the people I'm talking about

PENETRATED INTO THE DREAM
where the family sat around
a bonfire performing complicated music
with long silences
the two-lane highways of the dream
curved into the forest they never
reappeared a large shape
most like a thoughtful man
floated overhead while I rowed
us to the center of the lake
to enter its green waters
and suspended there
drink beers
at night the sky contained
the plans to continue

Feathery wood fiend
I found you
playing a violin
in the forest
the Great Lakes
were almost empty
I walked out
with my nephews
to the middle
of Lake Huron
during the recession
the gantries
were terribly sad
playing a song
with the wind
the useless lighthouses
cost one dollar
to feel them
swaying all alone
except one ghost
still feeling useful
lighting the lamps

FAMILIES SHARING MUSIC
WITH EACH OTHER
and drinking beer
in the hurricane
there's nothing else
they can do
power lines falling down
onto the restaurants
no pizza toppings
no letup
in the wind
that is like
a moth's cough
in the universe
and their songs
in the blackout
are like wind
they move on
eventually becoming wind
but the songs
for a moment
are a dress
the wind wears

YOUR DIRTY LITTLE BEARD
IS LIKE A RUNWAY
that's been bombed
by the Empire to prevent
the rebels using it
she said with her hand
firmly on my shoulder
exerting as much pressure
as one can without
being either mean or provocative

It was as M would say
The Pressure of the Real
much too real,
her face was set
in a mask of
The Day Is About to Break Upon Us
with Rain and in her eyes
a little tropical storm
surged over the shore.

YOU CAN'T HAVE 2 POWER SOURCES
IN YOUR CAR BECAUSE THEY WOULD
INTERFERE WITH EACH OTHER
you have to choose the one
that suits you best
either *Sobbing*
or *Sun Shining on the Desert*
both will get you where you are going
though there are many ways
to go and you don't
even have to think about it
the sun continues to punish us
beneath it somewhere someone
is still sobbing in fact
if we knew exactly how many people
were sobbing on Earth right now
we couldn't stand it
we'd be up off the couch
the cat knocked to the floor
and out to the streets
to tear out our hair

A MUNDANE HIDEOUT
from the day
a frayed rug
a window fan
papers lying around
books in disarray
on the shelves
a crocodile pipe
to your lips
your beautiful lips
opening with mine
like a mammal
from the sea

I CREATED THEIR CAREER INFORMATION FOR THEM

and this is how they paid
me back: they didn't even

understand me. I made it so clear.
I made a little program

with graphs and Venn
diagrams. Which are useless.

Those are for amateurs.
But I thought they'd like it.

When they came in the office
they started punching

the pillows on the couch.
They leapt around.

They screeched at my graphs.
And I realized they weren't

even capable of speech.
They weren't even wearing clothes.

They were covered in fine
pelts that changed color

slightly in the breeze.

I ONLY SMOKE CIGARETTES
ON YOUR ROTATION

everyone else sees me
as the actual smoke

passing in front of their
selection in the vending machine

or waving frantically
to get their attention

while pulling apart
in the afternoon breeze.

When I wake up in your bed
hungover, shredded cheese

in the bedclothes,
I always feel, briefly,

a terrible panic
that I never called home

with my excuses. But
you are my home.

I'll slit your barrel
and drink your wine
again tonight with you
tied up in sheets
Sunday night in September
the fan finally off
your wine's own chill
filling up the air
with your delicate smell
my head already pounding
and tomorrow morning waiting for me
to join it there

DRAGGING A METAL THING
RIGHT TO YOUR FRONT DOOR
and calling you down
into the wet grass
with my loudest whisper
every night this summer
that adds to my allure
I dragged this thing
right up to your threadbare sweater
that smells a little bit like nutmeg
from here I stage the assault
on your clavicles

THE BEST THING SHE KNOWS
ABOUT GOING TO BANKS
IS WHERE THEY ARE. Beyond that
she submits to a mystery.
It is an awful row of storefronts
on a very loud street
without trees.
The sky is a television news show
that can't be turned off. The money is
all in ghosts.

REDISCOVERING THE BABY'S
LECTURE PRESENTATION
filled me with sadness.

I never paid attention
in those days to a baby
on a dais

speaking of the origins
of English Romanticism
in the French Revolution

squandered by Wordsworth
and Coleridge, taken up again
by an untrustworthy Shelley

drinking a lot with classmates
filling my time
though now I can't imagine

how I did, no politics
no children, the internet
still a national secret

it was like gorging on magic
marshmallows—
the hangover is an even
deeper emptiness

IF YOU EAT THIS COOKIE
I WON'T LET YOU INTO PARADISE.
That is what
the whole thing comes down to.
I feel the late-summer breeze
slipping in under
the heat of the day.
Everyone wants to put
their stamp on that. I walk
through the crowds of people
with coins instead of eyes.
I know they don't see
me in league with scrubby
trees, passing notes to gulls
to pass on to the sea.

AUTHOR'S NOTE

THE SKY CONTAINS THE PLANS is a hypnagogic project I worked on for almost all of 2010. The hypnagogic state is that state of being between falling asleep and being asleep, when the mind becomes elastic and one either sees or hears odd, hallucinatory things. I noticed that I heard different voices, and what fascinated me about them was that they were almost always saying extremely mundane or lame things, not the exciting dream-world revelations one might expect. I also was interested in how unlike my own conscious writing these phrases were; so many of them were things I'd never write in a poem. Making these awkward lines into the opening lines of poems seemed an exciting challenge. So I trained myself to wake up from this brink of sleep and write (sloppily, sometimes sadly illegibly) in a notebook each night what the voices told me, and these became the first lines of these poems.

This first step, collecting the lines, took almost a year. I didn't write any of the poems until after I'd gotten 100 lines.

I tried to make the poem retain any form or rhythm the opening lines suggested.

I tried to enjoy myself.

AFTERWORD

ALL POETRY IS COLLABORATION

After writing a lot of poems, and doing a lot of collaborations, I have come to believe that the writing of all poems is a form of collaboration. A poet collaborates with another voice, or other voices. Those voices can take many forms, and are always there, if the poet is listening.

*

There are the collaborations everyone thinks of, where two poets write together, shaping a poem from the collision of their voices. I have done a lot of these. Joshua Beckman and I worked together for several years writing literally thousands of little poems, spoken together into a recorder and later transcribed into a homemade chapbook made on two typewriters in Staten Island—Birds Follow Mommy, it was called, and we sold them at our first collaborative performance at Bar Reis in Brooklyn. Later we published a book of them—Nice Hat. Thanks. We also did an audio CD of these— sometimes recordings of live, improvised collaborations, sometimes recordings of us making poems together, privately, driving around or sitting in the park.

*

These poems in The Sky Contains the Plans are collaborations with the voices I heard on the brink of dreaming. I took their strangeness, or sometimes their mundaneness, and I took the energy of that and used it to shape these poems. I let my voice entwine with these voices, and I let these voices show me where the poem was going.

*

Were all these voices my voice? Or were some of them voices I'd heard and stored unknowingly? I'm not sure, I haven't done the scientific research into it, but they sure function as another voice. They were as strange, and estranged, as can be.

*

I learned so much about my own writing, collaborating with Joshua. Having his voice exactly as present in my mind as my own voice while writing poems for several years both enriched my process and made me very aware of what it was that my voice added. Some nights I feel like the poems I'm writing now, quietly on my couch while the family sleeps, are still collaborations—either with Joshua or with an objectified, removed, nearly estranged version of my own voice.

*

Later I collaborated with Bashō, Buson, and Issa. I missed working with Joshua; he had moved away from Brooklyn. I was standing on the subway platform waiting for a train, feeling like I wanted to write a poem with someone else, to hear some other voice in my head too, and realized I had Robert Hass's anthology of haiku with me. I found some of their lines, threaded them with my own, and made a lot of poems together with dead poets. Their voices were there, waiting for me to respond, or swerve, or continue.

*

I've also written ekphrastic poems as long as I've been writing— one of my first published poems was inspired by a Joseph Cornell box at the Art Institute of Chicago, which I visited every time I visited my girlfriend. An ekphrastic poem is a collaboration with another source, obviously, but I've come to think of it as really being a collaboration with another voice, as well. A work of visual art is also someone's statement, or a gesture they've left us. It is a static form of their voice, their fossil voice. Writing a poem about or with a work of art is a collaboration with that original voice.

*

Collage poems and centos, too, are clearly forms of this, of using someone else's voice to get your own voice moving. I've written so many of these that sometimes I find an old poem and don't even know whether it was a collage with someone else or not. The method has become so natural, to listen.

*

I'm certainly not the first person to suggest that what a poet does is listen, but I'm saying it again. Joshua and I were invited to do a residency at MoMA which we called Eavesdropping. We spent about a month eavesdropping on the crowds in the different galleries, writing poems using their voices and our own, teaching children how to do this, and then performing these in front of the works of art where we'd heard them uttered.

*

Maybe I can't say ALL poems are collaborations. I guess I don't believe that. Some people just sit down to bang out their own beliefs furiously. But I think if we all thought of poems as collaborations with their *subjects*, we'd be less imperious about them.

*

The artist doesn't actually create anything. There is no creation out of nothing on this Earth. There's only making new things in collaboration with other things. Even the Haber-Bosch process of making abundant and cheap ammonia out of thin air is not creation out of nothing; it's making ammonia out of nitrogen and hydrogen.

*

And if we were more honest about our listening and our observing, we'd admit that what we're doing much of the time is collaborating.

*

Now Joshua and I collaborate in another way. When we get together, we want to share our new poems with each other. Our "own" poems. But what is my poem without his voice in it somewhere? How can I even know what I'm doing in a poem without that other voice there? So we read each other's poems aloud. I read him his poems (when they're typed; his handwriting is mysterious in the extreme). He reads me the poems I've written, and I hear, through his voice, if they've succeeded or failed.

*

I collaborate with the weather a lot in my poems too. I collaborate with the city. The city and the clouds and I work together on a lot of poems.

*

Some of my poems also remind me of what street photographers do. And what street photographers do is collaborate—with the city, with the citizens. There can't be street photography without the street, and the people who walk it.

*

I think the best street photograph is better than the best studio photograph.

*

One of the pleasures of THE SKY CONTAINS THE PLANS was writing so many poems. I love starting a poem, I love that energy that's present as something starts taking shape, starts coming together seemingly out of nowhere. And I love sharing that with another voice or other voices.

*

I am just laying out my weaknesses as a poet. Another weakness I have is I will try anything.

ACKNOWLEDGMENTS

Some of these poems first appeared in *Lit Hub* (thank you, Jonny Diamond), *N/A Lit Journal* (thank you, Amish Trivedi), *Pigeon Pages* (thank you, Kat Rejsek), and *Tupelo Quarterly* (thank you, Kristina Marie Darling).

My deepest gratitude to everyone at Wave—Matthew, Joshua, Heidi, Ryo, Blyss & Charlie. Thank you *"Falettinme Be Mice Elf Agin."*